JENNY SHELDON

LONGINGS

❧

Poems of a pilgrim

JENNY SHELDON

LONGINGS

∞

Poems of a pilgrim

MEREO
Cirencester

Mereo Books

1A The Wool Market Dyer Street Cirencester Gloucestershire GL7 2PR

An imprint of Memoirs Publishing www.mereobooks.com

Longings: 978-1-86151-673-2

First published in Great Britain in 2017
by Mereo Books, an imprint of Memoirs Publishing

Copyright ©2017

The address for Memoirs Publishing Group Limited can be found at
www.memoirspublishing.com

The Memoirs Publishing Group Ltd Reg. No. 7834348

The Memoirs Publishing Group supports both The Forest Stewardship Council® (FSC®) and the
PEFC® leading international forest-certification organisations. Our books carrying both the FSC
label and the PEFC® and are printed on FSC®-certified paper. FSC® is the only
forest-certification scheme supported by the leading environmental organisations including
Greenpeace. Our paper procurement policy can be found at
www.memoirspublishing.com/environment

Typeset in 9/15pt Bembo
by Wiltshire Associates Publisher Services Ltd. Printed and bound in Great Britain by
Printondemand-Worldwide, Peterborough PE2 6XD

With thanks to each one who has helped to form this pilgrim, especially to Mike, for our 50 years of journeying together.

FOREWORD

'God passes through the thicket of this world and wherever his gaze rests he turns all to beauty.' So wrote St. John of the Cross. Christian discipleship is a response to God's touch on our world and our lives. It is a response which begins in thanksgiving – in wonder, love and praise.

Jenny's poems reveal a life lived with thanksgiving at its core. Jenny's life has been rooted in prayer and steeped in the Scriptures over many years. This abiding in God releases her gift of creative writing. It is also the wellspring for her ability to see the everyday things of life with new eyes, whether it be the golden wings of the early-morning moth, the ticking hands of a grandfather clock or the anguish of human life heard in a radio interview. In Jenny's noticing of these things she follows in the footsteps of her Lord who stopped to see the beauty of the lilies of the fields, who gathered up the fragments of human suffering and who responded to the longing of the human heart. In the bustle of our fragmented 24/7 society we need men and women whose focus on God enables them to 'notice and name' where God's gaze rests, so that we too may see, and seeing may stop, may wonder and give thanks.

I am delighted that Jenny has felt able to offer her 'gift of contemplative looking' expressed through this beautiful creative writing. May it be a blessing to each person who takes time to stop, pick up this book of poems and ponder on the gaze of God.

Ann Coleman

The Reverend Ann Coleman has been a teacher, a spiritual guide, an enabler and a friend to me for many years. I have come to value highly her generous heart, her joy in God, and her wisdom which has helped me on many occasions. Thank you Ann.

ABOUT THE AUTHOR

Jenny Sheldon was born in Inverness but grew up in North Somerset, so as a child she experienced the joy of walking through lanes and fields to reach her junior school and the church she attended. Her love of the countryside and seascape deepened further when she went to a grammar school on the coast at Weston-super-Mare.

Then came a significant change in her life when she trained to be a nurse in London, where she fell in love and married Mike, a doctor. In the following twenty years Mike's work made it necessary for them to move home several times. For half of that time Jenny ran smallholdings, learning the art of goat-keeping, cheese-making and other skills under the tutelage of a greatly loved friend whose home was named Springfield.

In 1985 Mike, Jenny and their four children joined Youth With A Mission. They visited several countries, but most of Jenny's time abroad was spent in Uganda. Seven years later the family moved back to London and, significantly, to the East End.

Jenny taught Bible study before going to university and, having trained to be a priest, became part of a team in a Docklands parish. She also trained as a spiritual director and although Jenny and Mike later moved to Kent, she still works in East London.

She has turned to poetry as a way of expressing and reflecting the vastly varied life she has led. Some of the poems are rooted in her love of nature, the people she has encountered, and the spiritual journey that has led her and Mike to where they are today.

CONTENTS

LONGINGS

⤬

Beside the Way

MEMORIES OF SEASONS

I remember spring grass, green and tender
cut by cold March winds sweeping across fields,
a late fall of wet snow bending young branches
threatening to break their new-grown buds.
The persistent, burgeoning life of greening spring
struggles to free us from the clinging grip of dying winter.

I remember the summer smell of growth
warm, intoxicating, embracing, life-giving
the deep green shades of fully-leafed trees
sheltering cows from sun and flies
the foal in the field lying on its side
stretched out enjoying the warmth on its belly.

And in autumn the strangeness of trees I knew well
divided top from bottom by thick white mist, soft and still,
heavy crops of apples turned into fifty freezer recipes,
the inviting scarlet of hips, the prickliness of delicious blackberrying
the branch-bending fullness of elderberry bunches,
our rejoicing in provision given with such abundance.

Inevitable winter, bringing the shock of frozen water
unfallen leaves curled stiff by sparkling frost
trees standing stark, majestic in their barrenness
nothing left to hide until the soft silent snowfall
covers every branch like lint laid on a wound.
Nature is quietened, waiting, while we eat toast round the fire.

SUNFLY

Tiny sunfly dancing
bouncing ecstatically
in a pine-scented sunbeam.

Dance, dance, little fly
with your minute translucent wings
fluttering invisibly fast.

You ride the slightest breath
of the heat-heavy air
in a whisper of movement
that doesn't even touch my cheek.

I see you, little fly
living your day's life to the full
taking your shimmering space
smaller than my stretched-out hand.

I see you, little fly
filling your Creator's purpose
giving him glory, giving him joy.

Thank you for giving me wonder.
Thank you for his reminder
that I am made free, free to move
to dance in his Spirit's breath.

DARTMOOR LANES GO ON AND ON

The old stone walls of Dartmoor lanes
stand sheltered from strong winds and rains
yet keep their dampness in dry summer hours
to provide a home for ferns and flowers,
for lichens that cover the stones' hard faces
in greens and yellows, and some have traces
of red and brown and across these soft mats
if you look closely you might just catch
the greyish, crooked slimy trail
left by a night-wandering, day-hidden snail.
And growing above these miniature gardens
the hedge reaches high with promising burdens
of gin-seeking sloes and hazelnut twins
with their little green frills, and a few have skins
with a grow-fast stripe in a pretty pink
which in the autumn will be coloured mink
and be food for squirrels, or us if we're fast
and realise quickly when summer is past
and go nutting and brambling and gathering sloes
that give us warm memories in winter's cold.

These summer-full hedges with long leafy arms
invade open car windows – look out for the thorns –
but as we duck: watch out in front,
'cos we know we could always suffer a bump
for these car-squeezing lanes are too narrow to pass
and ten miles an hour is almost too fast   >>

and when there's a car that is zooming toward us
both must stop; the only way for us
is to give in and change to protesting reverse
till two of our wheels can bump up on the verge
and with a wave of the hand and a thank-you grin
the other driver's happy that we've moved in.

These twisting lanes, these leafy traps
overarching branches with so few gaps
feel claustrophobic, press in all around
shut out the view, the sights and the sounds
of the great expanses of glorious moorscape
until quite suddenly we make the break.

Sheep and ponies are quietly grazing.
Over vast hillsides great clouds are racing
and high overhead a buzzard is soaring;
this moor so dramatic, so alluring.

Lifting our eyes high to scan the grey tor tops,
these ancient, weather-worn granite rocks
we debate and decide which to conquer
in our two-hour-maximum mini-adventure,
for we're not as able as we used to be
we must count the cost, look to see
the ups and downs lest they get too steep
for our ageing joints now can't leap
'cross peaty streams, we can't risk a trip
on twiggy heather, we don't want to slip
on shiny bracken, but still we are drawn
through breathless uphills and wind-driven rain
to breathe this air, to follow the lure
of this very special magnificent moor.

LOSS AND DISCOVERY

(In response to a speaker's challenge to find beauty in our present surroundings. I found it through the windows of our home in Docklands; in Canary Wharf tower, the Amelanchier tree, the urban sunrise.)

In reflecting on your thoughtful words
I see the eye of my heart is dimmed,
glazed over with a veiling film;
I am caught by many fibrous roots
that cling to past soil. Weed unpulled,
plant unshaken, I am unable to break free.

Having been cradled in country beauty
I remember such awesome moments;
vast horizons of burning sunsets,
intense breath-holding of early morning,
still sleepiness of summer afternoons,
all-embracing silence of deep, deep nights.

But I have moved to urban surroundings.
Looking through different windows I must
cut free from roots that constrain me in my past
and search these present horizons,
closer, sharper-edged, full of fellow pilgrims,
to perceive the gifts of beauty that are here.   >>

The

view west

reveals an imposing

horizon of towers dominating

our sky. Yet in these bank-built

heights of steel and glass I see

reflections of awesome clouds

move in theatre over their face,

stormy shades of powerful greys

twisting and rolling, with edges

gleaming white, backlit by fierce

shafts of sun dancing in the sky.

A sudden roar assaults my ears

filling the threatening air above.

An urgent, throbbing sound that

powers the strident thrusts from

engines straining to gain height.

The noise grows less, and a dark

shadow demands attention as a

plane's shape leaves the tower's

earth-bound foot, climbs up the

shimmering transfigured wall of

glass and hard-edged steel, and

soars up, past the day-dimmed

flash of warning atop the glassy

pyramid. Higher and still higher.

Silent now, it fades towards the

distant curve of other horizons.

And I am left in wonder, seeing

the energy of westering sunlight

now transforming towered glass

into exquisite simmering beauty.

Looking east
through the window frame
I'm enraptured, captured by a glow
a burning of orange, tan, yellow, red
filling me with wonder at the intenseness
of its light, caught for perhaps one day only
every leaf hanging still, each in its own space.
The Amelanchier now in autumn glory
stuns with its beauty.
As it did in spring
over a few
short days
its delicate
canopy of
pure white
pristine
flowers
shone
bright
lighting
our room
then so quickly
fell to the sound
of the cold east wind.

>>

Early
in the dawn
of an equinoctial morning
the soft-eyed sun lights the east
waking the world to the vibrancy of day.
That same risen sun glares into our home
reflected from the mirrors in the west.
This double gift of God-created light
defies our gaze with brightness,
and brings me
hope.

Hope that wakens my heart to present beauty
to see that in this roofed and towered horizon
even here is revealed God-given creation.
And yet hush my heart, for there is more;
the call to recognise in my daily neighbour
the image of God, the likeness of beauty's Creator.

FROM THE FIRESIDE CHAIR

Springfield

Quiet, so quiet
activity distanced.
Becoming still
mind chatter diminished.
Growing awareness of
mellowed stone, shaped and honed
easy on the eye
bringing comfort to the heart.

Walls that hold, enfold, shield, protect
measured stones from rocks of ages,
soft-faced strength, forearm thick
give space to ancient leaded windows
that draw in the shortened day.
Interest awakened, question invited,
the heart is stirred to come and see
autumn framed in stone.

Leafless creeper trails and curves
the stony edge where man and nature meet.
A robin stands and silently sings
with all his red breast might.
Present son of many fathers
lights up this darkening year.

Shining beech leaves in glorious pendants
air-glowing gifts of gold and brown

>>

await the inevitable wind
that brings their final fall
to cover and enrich the earth
and feed their next year's show.

Poppy seed pods dry and stiff,
crown-topped vessels ready to be shaken
and scatter their seeds over damp-softened soil
beneath the old hydrangea heads
still blushing softly. Such subtle beauty
pleases the eye that sees.

Last flower of summer on faded stem
stands alone, bent and still,
its bright yellow petals still reflect
the flourishing life of summer gone.
One frail fragment breaks, and slowly falls
toward its winter bed.

Heady scent of autumn apples
carefully balanced in an old china dish
that sits secure in the windowsill's depth.
Fruit of a pip planted so many springs ago
watched, protected, nourished, gathered,
now enjoyed with the rest of harvest.

Walls not impervious to their surroundings
but through their pores draw into themselves
the breath-held stillness of summer sunshine,
the flickering wood of autumn firelight
spitting on the resin of barely dried logs.

These stones absorb the scents of nature
sun-kissed herbs and ripening fruit
for coming winter leanness.

These ancient stones, these steadfast walls
gather all together and bring to life
a wholeness seldom known
of earth and hearth, of trees and puddings
of weeding and eating, of patience and thanking.
These airs breathed in, breathed out
bring calmness, a peace that draws so many
towards its generous heart.

EARLY MORNING MOTH

Early morning moth
fluttering with golden wings among
summer-dried grass heads.
You signal the blessing of dawn-light
that has reached over the hills
to banish each tiny shadow
that lingered round my feet.
But as the sun grows fierce
you must fold your bright wings
and find your daytime hideaway.
And I? I shall follow your Creator's plan
and seek to dance in his light
to the tune that he has written
in the secret places of my heart.

TWILIGHT DAY

From Porthloo to Innisidgen, St Mary's, Isles of Scilly

The ruffled surface of the steel grey sea
merges into the dove-soft grey sky
absorbing me into its mistiness
bringing horizons closer
softening the edges of rock and island.

All looks dull
and is easily set aside, hurried through
to reach the ease of a brighter destination.
Our minds so quickly shut out
the life hidden within the quiet beauty
of this twilight day.

But look again,
favour this place, this moment
with long looks, with attention from the
inner eye, the inner ear
and savour the abundance of gifts,
gifts that arouse wonder, delight,
and enrich our inner being.

Little waves thunder lightly
as they curl and break in their own steady rhythm,
unpressed by the swell of stormy seas.
They recede with a quiet swish
leaving behind their foremost edges
like disintegrating ruffles of old lace.

The waves, disguising their forcefulness
relentlessly creep up the beach
and seep into the footprints that mark
my lone walk on the dulled sand,
a perfect foil for the wet-bright colours
of scattered limpets,
highlighting the exquisite design
so precisely ringed around their pyramids.

In the twilight stillness
a sudden stir catches the attention,
a flock of silver birds takes flight,
cuts the still air with silent wings.
Flying low they weave their paths together
and as one drop to the ground
lost to sight among the pebbles.

Climbing the Down
the jagged teeth of distant rocks
softened by mistiness
lead the eye out to sea
where the Bishop stands
defying silent waves
pounding its solitary place,
its hard outline softened
as though veiled in gauze.

This light, this soft precious light
is infused with a golden glow.
Unlike grey inland days
that weigh down, this air

uplifts, reveals a sea-reflecting glory
that creates a quiet atmosphere
of lingering time,
its moments and its hours unmarked
by the hidden arc of the day's guardian.

My silent footsteps fall
on soft needles beneath
brooding pines that flank this
northern shore. No sigh of wind
stirs their aged branches
as they stand sentinel, watching
tides rise and fall against the Men-a-vaur.
And at Innisidgen their line stands back,
a semicircle marking the ancient grave.

This twilight day is merging quietly
into night, and I must return
to shut out the softness
of this day where I have found
gifts to wonder at,
gifts that have become woven into my story,
for I have heard a different rhythm
seen a different light
moved in another dimension.

SPIRIT WIND

Wydale

This lovely valley
where the air is full of summer stillness
draws my soul into its enclosed creation
removing city debris to another world.
And I can join the peace, and rest
in nature's sleep of scented warmth.

Suddenly a breath of wind
brushes my face and I awake, knowing
its sole purpose is to catch my attention.
So I am ready for the great dance as
God's Spirit moves through the scattered trees
disturbing their shaded depths.

One sky-filling tree
fully dressed in high-summer green
thrashes its branches
like arms wildly gesticulating,
its leaves lifted and twisting
laughing in the gust of his breath.

On through another he moves
inviting, enticing, compelling
its summer-strength leaves
to join his swirling dance
and so reveal their lovely petticoats
of underside silver.

>>

Birch branches sway before him
long, delicate, graceful,
waving loose-jointed through huge arcs.
His breath subsides for a moment
and the tree's heart-shaped leaves
hang quivering as he passes.

Nearby one small tree
remains unmoved, quiet
amid the wonderful wildness.
In this wind, in its own given place
it is sheltered. Its contented stillness
the more remarkable; not defiant
nor unteachable, it stands
as itself, waiting its own
time to dance.

The wind blows again
and even stately pine trees
move stiffly to his dance
giving just a little
like the aged caught up in a memory
move to a well-loved tune.

Along the densely-wooded hilltop
a Mexican wave bows
the heavy heads of gathered trees.
A magnificent roar of sound swells
demands attention and stirs
the seeing heart.

This is not the wind of change,
it is not the season for leaves
to turn to glorious colours and fall.
This time is for joyous response
to bend but not be broken
to join the dance before his breath.

CITY DAY

Morning star
before the first bright streak of dawn
you promise day,
you chase away the long dark night
and in my dark and heavy soul
you bring your light
that sends away the gloom of heart
the lonely weight of circling thought,
and gives me hope,
my Morning Star.

Noonday shade
relentless sun has worn the day
but you bring space
to step aside and rest awhile
to leave behind my crowded work.
Into this place of shaded air
you bring your peace,
and I can see the worried world
with different eyes,
my Noonday Shade.

>>

Evening breeze
whispering through the city trees
you bring relief
and change the drum of city noise
to softer songs of rustling leaves.
My soul is stilled by your cool breath
that brings you close
and turns the mind from ego trips
to restfulness,
my Evening Breeze.

Night-time rest
essential to the closing day
you bring the dread
that sometimes haunts my restless hours
the looming fear that I have failed.
I lay these troubles at your feet
and pray for trust
that in your loving steadfastness
you will stay,
my Night-time Rest.

THROUGH THE WINTER WINDOW

Wydale Retreat

My dear Lord
in these days, amid this gentleness
I don't want to seek you
with heart blinkered by my own plans,
for my expectations need refining
towards your desires, your timing.
Cause me to trust you that I may
come to know your very self.

Sharpen my inner senses
that I may be touched by each lengthened moment
to gaze at this soul-invading beauty
and so reflect the awesome stillness
of standing trees exposed in winter nakedness;
silent, stark
branches providing a resting place
for the dusting of snow.

So still, my dear Lord
like a breath held in wonder
on the brink of morning.
Still, like noonday windlessness
as the sun hovers low in its winter-blue.
So still
like the moon hanging in the empty sky
like silence after Communion.

>>

Stillness, that allows an inward smile
a skin-tingling awareness
that in these days, this gentleness
it is good to wait for you my dear Lord,
to know the wonder of your coming
your presence that doesn't ask for trappings or traditions
but pours out the height, breadth, depth of love
for love's sake alone.

POEMS FROM WEST COUNTRY HEADLANDS

THE STIRRING

I have been
where the thrift blows dry
and glistens in the sun,
where the ling grows low
stands firm in the wind,
where the sea surges green
churning light and milky
swirling dark with mystery.

And my soul is stirred
awakened, enlarged,
embraced and at home
in this living melody of wonder.

THE TOP

Wind chinks the dangles on my jacket
finds every unprotected crevice
and it's a mad, exhilarating
blown-wild hair day.

The veil of sea rain
driven over spraying summits
of storm waves, envelopes,
fierce, hard, cold.

It will stop,
the sun will come to dry and warm
strong through brilliant blue, through cleansed air.
This creation is so very good.

WILDNESS

Wildness and wilderness
inclusion and exposure
watchfulness against footslip
elation, being within
the sea, the wind
this wild world on the edge
this lone freedom
this fear, this awe
all feed my soul.

THE EDGE

Crashing waves hurled onto cliffs
water against rock
rock against water
twice a day, every day,
being thrust upon and withstanding
being lit up by rainbows, bathed in watery lace
smoothed into sun reflectors
or broken in jagged crags;
creation and creature, formed
by the hand of beauty.

TIME IS BLOWN AWAY

And I have climbed
the long steep stepway
left behind wheels and windshields
notices and nurtured gardens
climbed up to walk the ridge
along its path that leads out into the sea,
walked into the west wind that blows
always, caressing roughly the shiny grass
and the wind-worn, foot-worn rocks
that lie low and comfortable,
yielding crevices for tufts of tiny thyme
pulsing its purple agedness.
And time itself is blown away
unknown and unconcerned.

JUST THE TWO OF US

Carefully we place our aging feet on the shared path
walking this narrow land, alive and honed
through sea and wind, sun and rain,
and his walking stick whistles in the wind.

Silent in the union of so many shared years
enjoying the togetherness, sharing the loneliness
embraced, quietened in these given moments,
but his walking stick still whistles in the wind.

We sit side by side on the stone slab
wondering at flowers of survival that kiss the low rocks
and the clear air, the distant hills,
and his walking stick lies quiet in the wind.

LONGINGS

❧

Fellow Pilgrims

EMERGENCY

with a friend in A&E

Time disrupted, disjointed,
time lengthened, shortened,
unreal time,
out of touch with the world outside,
this small, intense, personal place
of suffering, of unknowing.

Time out of my hands
dependant on other's decisions,
actions, inactions,
frustration of non-communication,
humility of dependence.
The temptation to please authority
to give self away in order
to have body restored.
The immediate invasion
of life-measuring machines
urgently bleeping
to record physical facts,
while the heart lies bleeding,
anxious breathing, unrestful body
torn between hope and fear,
losing and grasping,
and the waiting, waiting, waiting.

A FRIEND'S GRANDFATHER CLOCK

Springfield

Time ticks timelessly
in this home of sixty years.
Pressing times following times
after times, living and loving
birthing and dying.

Time ticks on timelessly
in this dream brought to reality
the hope, the struggles,
the challenges of life that's tough,
building through time.

Time ticks on timelessly,
the iron fire clicks as
flames burn to embers,
and long-tailed tits tap, t'tap-tap
on the twilight window.

Time ticks, timeless,
and I breathe the air
aware of another world
that touches this,
that gently touches,
like eyelashes on a cheek,
like a butterfly in the hand,
touching that fire within
that is a gift from elsewhere,
hinting of homing
with God,
when time no longer ticks
and is complete.

THE VISIT

Springfield

Treasure home of memories
so rich, so vivid, so present,
memories built through the long years
of a passionate, joint love of this chosen place.
Memories whose cords are pulled
by a chairside book, an autumn apple,
a carefully-treasured newspaper cutting.

As sweet spring water from the well
these memories draw from a deeper source
so deep, it stretches back beyond my knowing.
The story of two lives, two loves,
covenanted strength of lifelong promise,
steering the same plough, turning the straight furrow,
complementary partners in the same vision.

Memories, now sharpened by absence,
make them rich, make them vivid, make them present,
wonderful tribute to one so beloved,
perhaps softening the sharp cleaving of oneness.
Grief needs to remember,
to preserve the fruit of each heart-held treasure,
gifts that pave the future to your together home.

LEAVING HOME

Now you've gone.
You went so quickly
left so lovingly
grief and love expressed
in a long hug
that measured the long years
of child, youth, adult,
mountains and valleys
joys and reliefs
sorrows and challenges
that living and growing bring.

And yes, you have gone
to a new stage
the next step
that will last to life's end.
A good step
that through the years to come
will bring greater things.
Our years together
are now foundation and springboard
soil and roots
that loving and growing form.

Oh yes, I hurt,
my heart's pain
central and sharp,
the inside cry
that I try to hide,
and yet no desire

to keep you by
to hold you back,
just the realisation
that this grief
is good.

I who have watched and waited
now release and send
into the known
and the unknown years.

And my son
may God
who gives life and joy
who knows all pain,
bless you and keep you,
guide you and your love
till both lives end.

Daughter, child could be used instead of son

A PRAYER FOR YOUR SUFFERING

No more whys.
Quieten the questions.
Let go the search
the need to know.
Before the agonised face
of so much suffering
bow low
bow very low
and pray,
pray that somewhere
somewhere in the vast unknown
he will keep your life-light burning.
He will keep
and not let go.

TRIBUTE TO A FRIEND
Springfield

In this house, womblike with age
protective stone mullions,
their narrow panes hung with soft red velvet,
give glimpses of winter twigs
trying to invade the warmth and stillness
of this place within,
trying to reach the burning logs in the iron stove
to climb the worn oak stairs,

twigs that rock out of time with the slow tick tock
of unmeasured moments.

In this passing world enclosed
you gladly shoulder the daily tasks
of living away from the crowd.
No goading adverts, no grasping of status
dislocates
the peace that is here.
Through years of joy and courage,
tears and patience, you have nurtured the good,
nourished harmony, still welcoming as gift
all who come.

As you walk your day-closing rhythms
I sit here, quiet, waiting
and receive peace,
not just the peace of absent noise,
not the peace of having fought and won,
but a deep down, intimately invading peace,
a peace that gentles
calms the anxious turbulence of a busy mind
quietens the buzzing of a pressured heart,
and fills the whole.

MISSING YOU

On Retreat

It's a miss-you awakening.
As the morning dawns to break the darkness
and herald a day of new fullnesses
I long to hear your voice. And yet I know
I should be here; you should be there.

It's a miss-you morning
for in the space between activities
my heart calls for attention to its
you-shaped emptiness
not to be falsely stuffed with replacement fillings
but known, accepted, embraced.

Reflective afternoon
knowing I need to face your absence.
Pearl from grit; gold from crucible
pain edged with light as I give thanks to you
my friend for life; thanks to God for the gift of you
the gift of us.

Together we have seen
such wonderful views on the world from high mountain slopes.
And we have known deep valleys
where sorrow, pain and hurt
have chiselled away proud edges and brought
acceptance, a more knowing love.

>>

So thank you, my greatest friend
my closest companion, my steadfast supporter.
And thank you to God who undertakes, undergirds
who undoes the knots
and in whom all our future is held.

FRIENDSHIP AND MORTALITY

Springfield

How many more months do we have?
To sit, to have quiet conversations,
to enjoy the calm presence of this place
to be restfully contained by the fullness of all that is here
and yet somehow expanding our souls
through friendship.

Just one little word provides the entrance
to years of memories, of growth-giving times
when we have been together,
exploring the practical details of our land caring, family nurturing lives,
sharing the delights – and difficulties – of having husbands, being wives,
of children grown and growing.

This friendship, this intimacy, this companionship
our walking alongside
has deeply enriched my soul,
has sown and grown so many of the flowers and fruits within me,
has helped me write, helps me sing
the songs in my heart.

FULFILMENT

Springfield

The great gift of you, our togetherness
has passed. Such full memories
deep, deep in my heart. Such gratitude
I cannot express. These will endure
for the rest of my life here.

Thank you, heartfull thanks to you my friend
and to the One who accompanied us.

LOSS AND GAIN

Time ticks on
each quiet minute measured.
The chair opposite is empty
but still bears the impression of him
who sat for many hours
and has now moved on
finished the sufferings of his pilgrim life
and is healed. But for me
time still ticks on
and his absent presence
draws me into a gateway
an awareness that I am granted a touch
of something beyond,
timelessness,
where measured minutes stand back,

>>

a pause in time and place
in mind activity, in heart's grief.
A sense of calm joy, of awe;
the unknowing of the indescribable
and yet the assurance that all is well.
A fullness of being
where outer and inner senses are one
united in these unmeasured moments
these moments that transcend
the limit of my earthly life.
A gift to hold, a remembrance
to keep through time.

HEALING

From my shivering bed
I can hear your gentle voices
murmuring
and I am comforted.
Close friendship talk of many years
unconstrained by mobile minutes
continues its musical phrases
weaving like a low chant
filling me with quietness.

REMEMBRANCE

You have died.
The body I saw is dear
and yet it now no longer limits you.
The grief that pierces my heart
is for me, for my loss.
Deeper is an awareness
a knowing of great joy
a joy that is deeper than my grief,
an assurance given.

My sorrow is selfish sorrow
and yet it has, and will have, a place
in the process of letting go
of adjusting to life without you.
The given joy is received with thankfulness,
thankfulness for long sufferings ended,
thankfulness for the patient endurance that grew,
a portrait of grace and tenacity.

May I, in my sorrow
recall the good,
the grace of the sudden slipping away,
the Bible notes kept by until the end,
the words of those who lately knew you
building the portrait of
a gentle and loving man for whom they held respect,
your grateful smile of recognition,
your gratitude for care they were giving.

A springboard for treasured memories
of a good life now ended,
and yet newly begun.

RADIO INTERVIEW

Today I came near death.
Or did death come near me?
My listening was sharpened
attentive to every inflexion
I was drawn into the waves of a gentle voice
speaking of a terrible, shocking loss;
her husband died
suddenly, unexpectedly
no time to prepare
no time for care or goodbye.
The loss was dreadful, heart rending,
she spoke of grief indescribable
part of her lost forever,
their growing together
their sharing of life
vibrant with hopes and dreams
violently shattered.
No anger, no wishing, no dreaming,
no lonely weeping, no calling to the shadows
could make him return.

In older age this natural tearing apart
of two who have become one
is mind, heart, life challenging.
But when two are younger there are no words

only emptiness, intimacy torn away,
the soreness of open wounds in all the heart senses
and after timeless weeks
trying to grasp the painful challenge of living a different life
through the loneliness of the long road ahead,
every hour, every day carrying a sense of loss
as grief lives on to life's end.

I felt a forceful reminder that at times
each of us walks in the valley of the shadow of death;
perhaps not my own, that may be easier
than losing a life partner, one so closely beloved,
when a long road together becomes a pathway alone.

And where is hope in this?
Where is the light in this dark place?
It must be in the One who shares our grief
who has led the way
whom death could not hold.

LONGING

I love one
whose busy life allows
so little time for entente;
my heart pain grows.

The greatest love
is to hand over our shared
and unshared spaces to God
who loves most.

>>

And then in love
wait
and do what comes
to heart and hand.

IN REMEMBRANCE

For a Requiem Mass

In remembrance we have received
his body given, once, for all,
his body taken, blessed, broken, shared
sacrament of healing
a gift of grace that makes us whole.

In remembrance of him
whose body was broken
for our suffering, our pain
our failures in love,
in the mercy of God the compassion of Christ
walks with us the human road, and knows,
love's acceptance of human brokenness
all gathered into him, and he bore it to death.

As we gather to remember
John who has just passed on
we touch a doorway, a different dimension
a breaking-in of heaven, and we know
Christ's still-scarred hands held out to receive John,
the still-scarred feet gladly walk to meet him,
Christ's eyes shine with welcoming love

for a place has been prepared,
a home for rest eternal
and he is enfolded in peace
beyond our perception.

And our sorrow of loss
is shared with certain hope,
hope unshakeable, unmovable,
founded on God, alive in the Son,
empowered by the Spirit,
and in this hope we can pray:
May he rest in peace, and rise in glory, Amen.

change name as required

93RD BIRTHDAY

Springfield

You are older now.
Since we last met –
not so very long ago –
your body has aged,
is more stooped, more unable to respond
to help its own needs,
frustrating and frustrated as you must
give up so many little everyday activities
that in your active years have cared,
have given, striven to serve us.
Now you need others
to help care, to serve.   >>

This humiliation of need
turned right
grows a humble spirit
a joy to be with,
a wonder.

For ageing is an inevitability
that will surely come
and with you I am brought
face to face with disturbing reminders
of my own wearing into dysfunctions.
And I wonder,
how will I cope, bear with
the care that will be needed
as increasing disabilities
demand more attention,
asking me to give up minutes,
hours, and even days
of choosing my own way,
being in control of my own body,
– and soul?

And maybe there's the plan.
In you I see more wholeness
for you have found the balance
of self-care and self-giving,
but even as it's gained it slips away
in the presence of yet another change.
And you must seek again the wisdom,
the courage, to live.

For your heart yields daily, hourly to him
who gives you life. Your mind remembers
his years of caring, of loving,
of giving. And now the ageing
is understood, unsought
but accepted.

And so we come, wanting to be with you.
We see your eyes, at times in pain,
but so often sparkling as you tell
the stories of his love, his grace.
For he has slowed his walk
to be beside you. His quiet talk
is recognised, heard,
received into an open
and gracious heart.

O my God, help me to follow,
help me to be aware now
of how to face the inevitability,
not with fear or refusal
but with a quiet spirit
that will walk the slower path,
that will be teachable,
trying to find its own balance
of self-care, self-giving.
So that what I have loved, have watched
may live on, and be shared again.
Your kingdom come.

LONGINGS

Constant Companion

LOVE UNQUENCHABLE

The fire burns
lit by you,
kept by you
your fire burns.

Flames leap higher
desire reaches toward you
and some of your flames
burn my dross away.

It's all the same fire
lit by you
flames fanned by you
your fire that I contain
and learn to embrace.

THE JOURNEY

A sky-filling sense of you calls me
draws me, lures me on and on
to a tryst of your choosing.

Vulnerable love, poured out
is so joyous, so glad, so blessed
that your beloved's foot is on the path.

Arms stretched horizon-wide, your presence
welcomes in every place of waiting, and yet
goes ahead as each stage is journeyed.

Giver of courage to face the unknown way, the unknown end
Herald who has guarded the pitfalls, parried the darts of fears
Conqueror in love, so love can respond

and be led to where…

Lover surrounds, embraces, quietens
fills every part of this beloved's being.
And when she can at last

look into her Lover's face
I see such steadfast, steadfast love,
enough for all the path that is to be.

GOD APPROACHES

God comes arms outstretched
to hold, to comfort.
I shrink back
unable to fully go
unable to fully engage.
He waits patient and understanding
holding me in his gaze
loving me in his acceptance
just as I am.
He breathes,
I see, I like,
I know, I love.
How can I let go, let God?

God stays, arms wanting,
relaxed, at ease.
I turn to him
struggling to set myself aside,
wanting to embrace him.
He waits patient and understanding,
still, holding me in his gaze,
still, loving me in his acceptance
just as I am.
He breathes again,
I see, I like,
I know, I love.
I see the cost in his open palms.

God, God himself, my God,
moves closer, gently,
reading my opening heart.
I move towards him
desperate to engage, to be embraced.
He enfolds, his warmth, his love
so gently, so strongly holding
giving me all I want
just as I am.
He breathes I love, I love,
my love, my love
nothing can separate us.

THE SHARED CUP

I hold up the cup
of your suffering,
the crucible
that contains you now.

May God be seen
in the gold he surely holds
in the cup
of his scarred hands.

DANCING PARTNER

Today
may I dance with you,
so close
that I can see your eyes
    looking,
    with joyful love,
    so clear
    that I can see their depth
        knows,
        knows all my inmost being,
        my very core,
         all light and dark, all shades of grey
    perceived.
    Yet still you gaze
    and gaze,
    till I can see deeper, deeper,
        beyond
        all human understanding,
        beyond,
        beyond the bars of my own discordant tunes.
Today
may I know your arms
around,
feel your determination
    to hold
    with unshakeable strength
    my trembling
    that I may be assured,

certain,

we face every step, each twist and turn

together,

heaven's dancing partner at home in me.

FROM POVERTY TO RICHES

Retreat at Wydale

Through the sleepy summer trees

a moving whispers,

whispers in the sounds of leaves

rustling, like receding waves

drawing stones to the sea.

It lingers

moving through my soul, touching with presence,

helping me cry the tears so long held back,

causing to flow the frets and fears

that make me ache with tension.

Blow again Lord, blow,

blow far away these frowning thoughts,

this well-learned lesson that shrouds my soul,

wraps me tight in self-protection,

paralyses my inner life

in a winding sheet,

driving me to hide, and furtively watch

through jagged eyes of warped vision,

feel painful stabs from everyday conversation.

What poverty, what desperate poverty

is so exposed.

>>

A bruised reed you will not break,
a dimly-burning wick you will not put out.
You rent the heavens to come to earth
to face the depths of crucifixion.
You heave earth up to heaven
in the heights of resurrection.
And now, even now
you steadfastly blow your freedom breath
around the dim burning of our loves.
Blow Lord, blow, blow
that I might know the breadth,
height, depth, the never-ending riches
of your redeeming love.

Isaiah 42.3

THE STRUGGLE

A word someone spoke
caught the edges of my attention;
wounding word, unwelcome, unwanted.
I turned away – not possible,
not what I want
not what I can cope with.

And yet, there is a place of
No . . . . but?
The heartache, the struggle with fear,
with the unknown,
being stretched outside the zone
of my everyday security.
And then, there is a place of
a quiet Yes . . . . but?
Maybe I can, just maybe, maybe.
Problem becomes potential
of new horizons
and still I count the losses
can figure them so easily.

And yet
I have never known you do me harm,
never has your way been wrong.
There must be more than I can see
now, more than I can know
now.

>>

And yet
so much of me aches with losses,
they burn so deep, from deep within
my inner being they cry out
in pain.

And yet
I believe you hear, you know,
you must understand?
Still you lead on
this path I have not sought.
And I have a glimmer
that this may be your way
your refusal to let things stay
just as they are.

For you are life, burning, bursting life,
full life, abundant life,
invitation to life.
The gauntlet laid down.
Can I take it up?
Can I walk the shadows ahead?
Can I go where I have not gone before?
This road looks lonely and I feel unprepared.
But my judgement may stand up
against yours
and that cannot be.

So help me God.
For now I can say

but . . . . Yes
and offer up
the struggle, the tears,
the fears, the longing to know
your love, your acceptance
of my indignant, fearful
clenched fists.

So help me God.
So help me God.

REFLECTION ON JOHN 13

Jesus washed the feet of Judas.
As he knelt down, did their eyes meet?
What love flowed from Servant to betrayer?
Was there one last appeal
one moment in time offered
from the one who already knew
the dark potential in this disciple's heart?
This appeal of love so misread, so misunderstood
interpreted in the darkness of his own purpose
in the heart that turned
to go out into the night.

Jesus washed Judas' feet.
How could you do that, Lord? How could you
kneel before the one who paved your captors' path?
Because you set your purpose like flint
cutting through life-saving distractions
to stride towards the turbulent city
of prophets' deaths, to face the uneasy alliance
of religious power and military might
that another kingdom may come and fill the world
with the power of life given
in sacrifices of love.

John 13.5-30; Luke 9.51

ALL OUR DAYS

All our days, all our nights,
life and death, death and life
around us, within us.
But when death comes close
life is more vibrant, more vital, more desired,
we tremble in the struggle to grasp
its potential elusiveness
its human uncertainty.
Only when we offer it up
is it given
in its fullness, its fulfilledness,
and we find faithfulness
waiting.

GIFT

Christ crucified
hung above the altar
broken body
given into paten
blood and water
poured into chalice
we receive
and are given new life.
Our brokenness
taken, received
blessed.

BROKEN BODIES

In hospital

I receive his broken body
right here, here among our bodies
broken by age and accident.
His body, precious, holy
sign of grace given
here amidst the pains, the fears
that tear us, body and soul.
His presence, so present
enters right into the heart,
is inseparably part of our suffering,
is intimate, deeply embracing
our broken humanness
in his broken body.
And I bow my heart in wonder
that what I knew in the distance
is now so near.

HE LOVED FIRST

I love because he loved first.
He loved, and would not hide his love,
would not withdraw. From his love's fire
he placed a glowing coal within my inmost self.
He cupped his hand around this spark of life
so my cold winter winds could not blow it out.

He gently blew with his eternal breath;
I felt an unknown warmth, a minute's melting
of the inner frost that gripped my heart,
that lay imprisoned in its house of ice
whose walls glisten and gleam with frozen strength:
and yet they must reflect this new flame's life.

And he stayed. He stayed within
guarding my inner hearth
where his new life was secretly cradled,
nurturing his gift with constant eye
lighting up with joy at every burst of brightness,
lighting up with love at my enquiring wonder.

And from that coal emerged a flickering flame,
uncertain, unsteady, so unready
for any stronger blow. But now he needed
both his loving hands to cup around
the fire, to shape his sacred breathing
that grew his flame

my flame, that now I felt more often.
And I began to know love, and love's care,

and I became aware of warmth, and of coldness,
of his ardent love, of my own unlove,
of his eyes' smile, and willing sacrifice,
a glimpse of his eternal breaking in.

THE CROSS

My God, my God
why have you forsaken me?
O my God I cry in the daytime
but you do not answer
and in the night
but you are silent.
You are my God
even from my mother's womb.
I am poured out like water
for the hounds are all about me
they pierce my hands and my feet.

So terrible it brings a sense of
unreality, for I cannot grasp its
terribleness, its darkest depths
its enormous offensiveness.
So terrible it has a weight of
absolute reality, its urgency
approaches, comes close
its horrible horror invades
my being, my self
and brings healing, brings peace
and this is the wisdom of God.

Psalm 22

MY LORD THE RUNNER

I will pursue you, running Lord,
I'll keep on running
running still whilst I can catch
just a glimpse of your dear shadow,
a thought, a hint of memory
enticing me on
firing my desire to pursue,
to run, to run through
whatever forms my path.

I will keep on running
following just behind you
running Lord, you who draw my love
to give strength in this pursuit.
I will not slacken pace
that I may at last
touch the fringes of you.

I will to pursue, running Lord
though mist clings and feet grow weary
I will to pursue, desperate to know you
more, for this is the seed you have sown.
I will to pursue you, dear running Lord
until I fall exhausted to the hard earth
and weep for my loss.

And I will wait, and wait, and trust that
in the nothingness that is left of me
you will come and having mercy
will embrace me with yourself.

MEDITATION 1

Body stilled
subjected to the alertness of my inner being
ready to enter his place
to set out towards a soft grey horizon
of misty hiddenness.
And the destination?
Is secure in his heart.

MEDITATION 2

Sailing out on an unknown sea of barely-moving water
not knowing where the wind will come from
where it will blow my boat,
but certain it will come
in little gusts or long blows
and it will not ditch me into the sea to drown.
For the sea is he who carries me
the wind is his messenger
and I shall land safely
a little further along the shore
I left behind.

MEDITATION 3
APPROACH

Deliberate steps over soft-hued pebbles
avoiding the clumps of still-glistening seaweed
aware of gulls crying their sad complaints
of wind blowing through salt-dried grasses
with a gusting shh ... shh ...
the touch of rough rock streaked with alabaster
wet where the waves have splashed.

And now the edge, the brink
where fluid meets firm
where half-visible depth meets certain footing
where waves curl and break with a finite splash;
carriers of change, of giving and taking,
heralds of the unknown.

INVITATION

The boat rope tightens and loosens
as the unseen strength buffets its mooring.
Prow trying to turn with the outgoing tide
is still held fast, agitating to move with the sea
to be caught up in the current
that will swirl it towards the unknowable.
Oars lie waiting, ready to be lifted to fend off
from the visible rock and the safe shore.

LETTING GO

Take care, grasp confidence, step into the rocking boat,
untie the rope and fling it inside the prow.
The boat turns, is caught in the outflow
and slowly floats away, settles, finds its place.
And then midstream is reached
we race with the massive force of purposeful current
and I am cut off from senses of land
caught into silence, the mystery
of deep, deep waters.

THE LOG AND THE CHIP

The fiery dart shot in
quick as lightning
it found its mark;
the old dry tinder
waiting to be set alight.

>That old tinder, a word heard
>its twisted meanings gathered over years
>so quickly sets the fire ablaze.

Crackling flames hiss and spit
their tongues break out
burn down my inner door,
violate my secret shadows
and ignite the hidden logs.

>Strange logs, elusive, threatening,
>sawn with the chains of self-defence
>undiminished survivors of past fires.

Fierce furnace heat
feeds simmering anger
expands it, compresses it,
turbulence of pressure whirls into tornado
desperate to find a way out.

                    My heart burns, my mind inflamed
                    works so hard to shift the blame
                    and yet another conflict is set alight.

Is this my path for our years to come?
Is this fire unquenchable, its fuel unconsumable?
Is there no relief from this haunting pattern
the blackened pains of past burnings
smothered with blankets of avoidance and fear?
Cooling drops touch my heart,
in the insistent flow I taste release
and turn, to see salvation poured
from love that gave complete.
Death-defying death, raised to
life-giving life, embraces my desperation
and I am healed.

Matthew 7.5

STARDANCE

Earthbound by anxieties
by obligation of 'must-do'
longing to stretch out mind, heart, body...

I heard your voice calling,
I looked around and couldn't see you.
Again you called my name
look up
and in the looking I am among the stars,
steady lights in the deep night
and distant earth a lovely glow of life.

We dance a dance of freedom
and here the part of me that can respond
is free to join your dance
of exuberant movement.
Whirling our way among the stars
we touch hands,
a shower of lights falls earthward.
As our footsteps move together
the heavens rumble with rejoicing.
Everything is still
and yet vibrates with life,
the only wind is from
our swirling togetherness.
This dance danced is an echo,
a reflection of eternity.
Our final laughing embrace
completes the dance.

And I am where I was.
No time has passed
but I am more,
the memory lingers
running like a thread
through my earthboundedness.

FINAL EUCHARIST

Retreat – final day

Roseate lilies turned to soft white petals
scattered before Christ the Teacher
symbol of a week-long flourishing
from the scents of Christ.
Gathered from the nations
to pursue him, to know him
to imbibe, absorb, to seek in one another
the Source of Love.

You call us, summon us
to carry your poured-out blessing
to a dried-up world
that hardly knows its thirst,
is unaware of its missing fruitfulness.

Keep us thirsty, keep us longing
to gulp down, draw up, to be drenched in
the fountain of life so abundantly gifted from
the Source of Love.

*Retreat Title: The Source of Love. An icon of Christ the Teacher and a vase
of lilies took centre place for this retreat.*